Share and Share Alike

A Musical Comedy

Geoff Morrow

A Samuel French Acting Edition

FOUNDED 1830

SAMUELFRENCH-LONDON.CO.UK
SAMUELFRENCH.COM

Copyright © 1985 by Geoff Morrow Music Limited
All Rights Reserved

SHARE AND SHARE ALIKE is fully protected under the copyright laws of the British Commonwealth, including Canada, the United States of America, and all other countries of the Copyright Union. All rights, including professional and amateur stage productions, recitation, lecturing, public reading, motion picture, radio broadcasting, television and the rights of translation into foreign languages are strictly reserved.

ISBN 978-0-573-08063-0

www.samuelfrench-london.co.uk

www.samuelfrench.com

FOR AMATEUR PRODUCTION ENQUIRIES

UNITED KINGDOM AND WORLD EXCLUDING NORTH AMERICA

plays@SamuelFrench-London.co.uk

020 7255 4302/01

Each title is subject to availability from Samuel French,

depending upon country of performance.

CAUTION: Professional and amateur producers are hereby warned that SHARE AND SHARE ALIKE is subject to a licensing fee. Publication of this play does not imply availability for performance. Both amateurs and professionals considering a production are strongly advised to apply to the appropriate agent before starting rehearsals, advertising, or booking a theatre. A licensing fee must be paid whether the title is presented for charity or gain and whether or not admission is charged.

The professional rights in this play are controlled by Samuel French Ltd, 52 Fitzroy Street, London, W1T 5JR.

No one shall make any changes in this title for the purpose of production. No part of this book may be reproduced, stored in a retrieval system, or transmitted in any form, by any means, now known or yet to be invented, including mechanical, electronic, photocopying, recording, videotaping, or otherwise, without the prior written permission of the publisher. No one shall upload this title, or part of this title, to any social media websites.

The right of Geoff Morrow to be identified as author of this work has been asserted by him in accordance with Section 77 of the Copyright, Designs and Patents Act 1988

CHARACTERS

Miss June Betterby, Headmistress of the Edwina Roach School for Girls
Miss Nelson, History teacher
Madame Souflee, French teacher
Miss Olden, elderly Deputy Headmistress

Class of 6C:
Jessica Lang, form captain
Cathy Burns, new girl from America
Susie Clements
Gill Thorn
Helen Fish

John Duff, local bank manager
Detective Sergeant Lawman, CID officer
Examiner
Extras

The action takes place at the Edwina Roach School for Girls

ACT I Scene 1 The school hall. The beginning of the new term
       Scene 2 The classroom
       Scene 3 Detective Sergeant Lawman's office
       Scene 4 Miss Betterby's office
       Scene 5 The teachers' common room
       Scene 6 The school hall

ACT II Scene 1 Outside the ballroom
       Scene 2 The classroom. Two months later
       Scene 3 The school hall
       Scene 4 Detective Sergeant Lawman's office
       Scene 5 The classroom
       Scene 6 The Examiner's office
       Scene 7 The classroom
       Scene 8 Miss Betterby's office
       Scene 9 The school hall. The last day of term

MUSICAL NUMBERS

ACT I

1	School Song	School
2	Something Will Turn Up	Miss Betterby, Miss Nelson, Miss Olden, Madame Souflee
3	Revise Revise	6C Girls, Miss Nelson, Miss Olden, Madame Souflee
4	Funny Lady	Lawman, Miss Nelson
5	Getting It Together	Cathy, Susie, Mr Duff
6	Going Round In Circles	Miss Olden
7	It's Easy	6C Girls

ACT II

8	We All Make Mistakes	Lawman, Miss Nelson
9	It's Stupid (*Reprise* of It's Easy)	6C Girls
10	Mr Examiner	Gill, choir
11	School Song (*Reprise*)	Jessica, School
12	I'm In Love, Mr Duff	Susie
13	Going Round In Circles (*Reprise*)	Lawman
14	Paris Paris	Madame Souflee
15	Can I Say Something?	Helen, 6C Girls
16	Sorry	6C Girls
17	School Song (*Reprise*)	School
18	Can We Say Something? (*Reprise*)	Company

The score is available on hire from Samuel French Ltd

PROLOGUE*

A Girl, or Headmistress of the School performing the play, comes on to the stage C and reads from this script

Girl This play is about a school.
The school is old, badly run and in dire financial straits.
The teachers ... well the teachers leave a lot to be desired.
The cast have asked me to point out most emphatically however that this is a work of fiction and bears no resemblance whatsoever to this school.
Thank you.

The Girl exits

---

*N.B. Paragraph 3 on page ii of this Acting Edition regarding photocopying and video-recording should be carefully read.

ACT I

Scene 1

The school hall of the Edwina Roach School for Girls

The girls and teachers are standing for morning assembly. It is the first day of a new term, and the headmistress, Miss Betterby, is addressing the school

Miss Betterby ... And so girls, I expect you to approach this new term with determination to succeed, and let us improve on last year's rather poor effort all round. This term, I want to see smiling faces——

The girls all over-accentuate forced smiles

—heads held high——

The girls forcibly jerk their heads up high whilst maintaining the forced smiles

—with eyes fastened on the goal ahead ...

With their heads still in position and still smiling, the girls open their eyes widely and glare ahead

As is our tradition, school, I want you (*pointing*) to regard the picture over there of our founder, Edwina Roach, to whom we owe so much, (*aside*) and can't afford to pay back! Above her portrait are some words which mean so much to this school. Some words that sum up the reason we are here. Those words are ... (*Screwing her eyes up to read*) "Susan Dingwell is a silly old——" (*Realizing*) The girls responsible for that disgraceful prank will report to my office immediately after assembly. No. The words to which I was of course referring are immediately above the portrait and read ... "THINK, DEVELOP AND LEARN." That, girls, is why we are here. So, remember every word I've said——

The girls adopt the forced pose above

—and let us take pride in singing the School Song.

Their faces now drop in disgust. The music for Song 1 begins

Song 1: School Song

School   We love our school, we thank our school
          For showing us the way
          To love our country and our Queen
          Yes caring day by day
          We chose our school to find the road

That leads to morning light
We love our school we thank our school
For teaching what is right

Counter melody sung against above

What a lot of old rot
What a load of old rot
We have to sing
Love our country and our Queen
What they're saying doesn't mean a single thing
We didn't chose this school we put up such a fight
We love our school, we thank our school
Let's burn it down tonight!

Miss Betterby looks down on the girls, smiling broadly

Miss Betterby Thank you girls. That was lovely. I always say there's nothing like our school song.

Girls And that was nothing like our school——(*They all giggle*)

Miss Betterby (*interrupting*) Thank you girls! Now. Miss Olden has something to say to you.

Miss Olden is old. She slowly and painfully makes her way to join Miss Betterby on the dais. As she moves she can occasionally be heard to cry "Oh dear! Oh dear!"

Miss Olden Oh dear! ... Oh dear! ... Oh yes. School ... I have to tell you ... Oh what was it now ... Oh dear! Oh dear! ... I had a piece of paper somewhere with it written down. (*Fumbling for it*) It was quite important ... Oh dear!

Miss Betterby Thank you Miss Olden! I think that what you are going to tell the school is about the special talk being given tomorrow by our local bank manager, Mr Duff.

Miss Olden Oh thank you, Headmistress. That's exactly what I was going to say. (*She pauses*) Was I going to say anything else?

Miss Betterby Yes. I think you were going to remind the girls that Mr Duff kindly gives up his time once a year to come to the school and talk about banking and finance.

Miss Olden (*excitedly*) Yes! Yes! That's it! What else! What else!

Miss Betterby (*trying to ignore Miss Olden's outbursts*) Well. I think that's all. I'm sure, girls, that you'll find the talk most interesting and exiting.

Jessica (*sarcastically*) Oh I'm so excited!

Susie Oh. How thrilling!

Helen How interesting!

Gill How will we live till tomorrow!

Miss Betterby Yes. I thought you'd be pleased. Right now. School dismissed. Good-morning, girls.

Girls Good-morning, Miss Betterby.

The girls file out to the accompaniment of the "School Song"

The CURTAIN *lowers leaving some of the teaching staff in front of the curtain*

Act I, Scene 1

Miss Nelson runs on and goes up to Miss Betterby

Miss Nelson Oh Headmistress, Headmistress! I'm so glad I caught you. I've just been to the book cupboard and the history books that I was promised aren't here *again* this term!

Miss Betterby I'm sorry, Miss Nelson, but the truth of the matter is that we did our sums and I'm afraid we just didn't have enough money for those new books. I know I promised that this term you would definitely have them but ... (*pleadingly*) could you make do with the old books for just one more term?

Miss Nelson Oh very well, Headmistress. But it is getting terribly confusing for the girls. A lot of them think that Queen Victoria is still on the throne.

Miss Olden (*speaking very low and sadly*) Ohhhhhhhhhhhhhh.

Miss Betterby What's the matter?

Miss Olden (*nearly in tears*) Did Queen Victoria die?

Miss Betterby (*ignoring the remark*) Look Miss Nelson. I'm going to make you a promise—and it won't be like any of my other promises—this time I mean it! Next term your books are going to be *top of my list*.

Miss Olden And oh dear! Oh dear! The girls are having such trouble playing hockey.

Miss Betterby Well, it's up to you, Miss Olden, to see that they practise.

Miss Olden Without hockey sticks?

Miss Betterby Don't worry, Miss Olden. Next term your hockey sticks will be on top of my list!

Madame Souflee (*who speaks with a strong French accent*) Miss Betterby. I must talk with you about the school trip to France this year. Last year we were really lucky with the weather, but I really don't think we can expect the girls to swim over again.

Miss Nelson I agree. Oh Miss Betterby. What are we going to do? The school building is badly in need of renovation; the playing fields are devoid of any grass and the roof of the music hut is so bad that I think we should change the school song to "Raindrops Keep Falling On My Head".

Miss Betterby Yes ladies. I know, I know. But I can promise you that all these things are right on top of my list. (*She pauses*)

The music for Song 2 begins

I don't know what the answer is, but I'm a strong believer in the adage that "Something Will Turn Up".

Song 2: Something Will Turn Up

(*Singing*) Whenever the odds are all stacked against me
And someone's ready to burst my balloon
I tell myself—until I believe it
Something will turn up, turn up, pretty soon.

Whenever it seems as though there's no answer
I keep on humming a pretty tune

And people suddenly start believing
Something will turn up, turn up, pretty soon.

They call me a perfect optimist
And maybe that's what I am
And being a perfect optimist
Things always run to plan

Miss Nelson   It's no good hiding your head in the sand you know
Miss Olden   The fact is, we've run out of money to spend
Madame Souflee   So maybe it's time that you stopped wishful thinking
'Cos will something turn up, turn up, in the end?

The three of them look across at Miss Betterby who is appalled that they could even dare ask such a question

Miss Betterby Something will turn up, turn up, in the end.

The Lights fade

SCENE 2

The classroom

When the CURTAIN *rises, about fifteen girls are entering the room. Some take their places at desks whilst others stand about in groups chatting. The attention of some girls is taken by a solitary figure standing at the door. One of the girls in the centre of the room is the first to speak*

Jessica Hi! Can we help?
Cathy (*slight American accent*) Yeh ... is this Class Six-C?
Jessica No. This is the set for the next Muppet Movie! (*After a pause*) Yes. This is Six-C.
Cathy (*walking in*) Hi! I'm Cathy Burns.
Susie Cath-y ... of course. We should have known from your accent. You're the American girl that's joining the school.
Cathy Well, actually I'm not American. It's just that I've been living over there for so long that I guess I've picked up an accent. But yes, I'm the new girl.
Jessica Well, welcome. We're sure you're gonna be very *un*happy here!
Gill Will you please tell me why any sane person would leave America to come to *this* school?
Cathy (*laughing*) Yes. My family came from round here originally. Then, about eight years ago, the company my dad works for asked him to go to the States. Now they've asked him to come back. The only school they could think of round here was the school my mother used to go to—this one. So here I am!
Susie Hard luck kid!
Helen Shame!
Jessica (*throwing her hands up in the air in despair*) What can you do?

Act I, Scene 2   7

Cathy Oh come on. It can't be that bad. I looked at the prospectus my mother had kept, and this school is certainly the best in the district. Do you realize that this school has more passes into university than any other school in the dis——
Gill What year is that prospectus?
Cathy (*unfolding and looking at the prospectus she is holding in her hands*) Oooooh ... nineteen forty-one. But the teachers, I heard the teachers were meant to be the cream, specially chosen for——
Gill Look. The only thing that's left of the cream are a load of clots! (*She turns to Jessica*) Shall I tell her—or will you?

The music for Song 3 begins

Jessica Pass me the timetable!

Song 3: Revise Revise

Jessica	First we have Miss Nelson, Miss Nelson is a bore
Susie	Exactly what she teaches, well none of us are sure
Gill	We hear she lost her lover in nineteen forty-three
Helen	The quicker that she finds him well the better off we'll be!

Miss Nelson enters and takes her place at her desk

Girls (*speaking*)	Good-morning Miss Nelson.
Miss Nelson	Revise! Revise!
Girls	Revise! Revise! She wants us to revise
	She thinks that we're not looking, gets her hanky out and cries
Miss Nelson	Revise! Revise!
Girls	We guess she doesn't know
	She took all our revision books away two terms ago!

The end of period bell rings. Miss Nelson, dabbing her eyes with a handkerchief, gets up and leaves the room still shouting "Revise."

After a brief moment Madame Souflee enters and sits at her desk

Girls (*speaking*)	Bonjour Madame Souflee.
Madame Souflee	Boujour! Bonjour!
Jessica	Now we have Madame Souflee who thinks she's "Ooh la la"
Susie	She tries to teach us French but isn't getting very far
Gill	She never speaks in English, I know it sounds absurd
Helen	But she just keeps on talking we don't understand a word!

During the next chorus Madame Souflee talks very rapidly in French to the girls whilst they sing

Girls	Bonjour! Bonjour! That's all that we can say
	But it seems to make her happy as she's jabbering away
	Bonjour! Bonjour! We lead her quite a dance

We're hoping that she'll pack her bags and jabber off to France.

The end of period bell rings and Madame Souflee, still jabbering away in French, gets up and leaves the room

After a few moments Miss Olden enters, knocking things over and crying "Oh dear! Oh dear!"

Girls (*speaking*)	Good-morning Miss Olden.
Miss Olden	Oh dear! Oh dear!
Jessica	And now we have Miss Olden, who's very old and slow
Susie	They say she taught Disraeli that was quite some time ago
Gill	We all know that Miss Olden had a promising career
Helen	But we get the impression she's forgotten why she's here!
Miss Olden	Oh dear! Oh dear!
Girls	She says it all day long
Jessica	The moment she walks in the room, well everything goes wrong.
Miss Olden	Oh dear!
Girls (*echo*)	Oh dear!
Miss Olden	Oh dear!
Girls (*echo*)	Oh dear!
	We just don't learn a thing
	And guess what she says every time she hears the school bell ring?

The School Bell rings

Miss Olden (*speaking*) Oh dear! Oh dear!

Miss Olden gets up and leaves the room still crying "Oh dear!"

Girls	Revise!
	Bonjour!
	Oh dear!
	Bonjour!
	We think that they're all mad
	Compared to other places though it isn't all that bad
	Revise!
	Bonjour!
	Oh dear!
	Bonjour!
	The good thing 'bout our school
	From Monday through to Friday we don't have to work at all!
	Revise!
	Bonjour!
	Oh dear!
	Bonjour!

Act I, Scene 2   9

> It drives us round the bend
> The question that we're asking though is where will it all end?
> Revise!
> Bonjour!
> Oh dear!
> Bonjour!
> The good thing 'bout our school
> From Monday through to Friday we don't have to work at all.

Cathy Oh come on now! Things can't be as bad as that?
Jessica No. Actually you're right. They're not. (*After a pause*) They're much worse. Look. I'm sorry I haven't even introduced myself. My name's Jessica. Jessica Lang, (*Pointing*) That's Susie Clements, that's Helen Fish ...
Helen (*extending her hand*) Hi! Can I say something?
Jessica No! Let me warn you about Helen. Given half a chance she'd talk from nine o'clock in the morning till nine o'clock at night—*and* rumour has it that she keeps talking all the time she's asleep! But to continue ... that's Gill Thorn and ... hey! This is crazy. Do I really expect you to remember twenty-odd names?
Cathy Well, despite what you say I've got a feeling that I'm going to be very happy here. With friends like you how can I go wrong.
Gill True!
Cathy Anyway. You've told me what to expect today but, what's this lecture thing tomorrow all about. Do we have to go?
Susie (*dreamily*) Oooooooooohhhhhh John Duff!
Gill Yes. Look! We apologize for Susie, but we have the same thing every year. You see I'm afraid she's hopelessly infatuated with Mr Duff from our local bank. (*Laughing*) But I'm afraid he doesn't show her any "interest"! But once a year he comes here, and once a year we have to put up with old Susie going into her daydream.
Jessica But the answer to your question I'm afraid is that "yes" we do have to go. A few years ago, as an experiment, Miss Betterby made it optional, but I'm afraid that old Duff spent one hour and ten minutes talking to himself about banking.
Cathy You're kidding me!
Jessica No, really. Of course Miss Betterby was there and a few teachers, but the next year of course it was compulsory for all girls to attend.
Gill He's actually not a bad bloke. But he *is* a terrible male chauvinst. He thinks that banking finance and the female sex just don't go together—as you'll hear no doubt in his lecture tomorrow. But we get the definite impression every year that he's just as bored talking to us as we are listening to him.
Cathy So why does he come?
Susie A very good question! For some reason I have never been able to understand, he happens to be potty about Miss Betterby. No accounting for taste I supppose!

Cathy How on earth do you know that?
Susie Oh, you can see from the way he looks at her. Also, a couple of the girls have been in her study when he's phoned her for a date. But she doesn't want to know. (*Sarcastically*) "The school is her life!" But this once-a-year lecture is a very good excuse for him to have to come to the school and talk with her.
Cathy And how long has this been going on?
Susie Too blooming long. (*Exaggeratedly*) Can't he see there are other fish in the sea?
Jessica Other fish! You're like a killer whale when you get going! But I'll tell you this. If he starts that chauvinistic attitude tomorrow ... oooh there'll be trouble! We'll show him we're not the female morons he thinks we are.
Gill What would you do Jess?
Jessica I don't know. But in the words of our beloved headmistress "Something Will Turn Up"!

The Lights fade

SCENE 3

The CID room at the local police station—Detective Sergeant Lawman's office

Lawman is seated behind his desk. There is a knock at the door

Lawman Enter!

Miss Nelson walks in

(*Standing and showing her to a chair*) Mornin', ma'am. Lawman's the name. Detective Sergeant Lawman, CID. Please take a seat. How can we be of help?
Miss Nelson Oh good-morning, Detective ... may I call you Detective for short?
Lawman (*puzzled*) Well, actually ma'am, perhaps "Sergeant" would be a little easier. "Detective" on its own sounds like I'm Sexton Blake or something.
Miss Nelson Sexton ...? Oh is he stationed here as well?
Lawman (*even more puzzled*) No ma'am ... he's a ... oh look it's not important. I am quite a busy man, so how can we be of service?
Miss Nelson Oh of course. I'm so sorry. And it's so nice of you to spare me the time. Of course I realize how busy you must be, I mean you've never out of the newspapers are you? ... Not you personally of course, but your ... (*she looks round searching for the right word*) ... company! You know I do admire the police so much. It fascinates me how you solve crimes and find things out. Where you get all your information from ... well goodness knows!
Lawman Thank you, ma'am. Now. I know that you were born in Swansea, you now live in Welgarth Road, you are a schoolteacher and you drive a blue Escort.

Act I, Scene 3
11

Miss Nelson (*quite taken aback; after a pause*) Well, there you are. that's exactly what I mean. That is quite extraordinary. Sergeant Lawman, how on earth did you get all that information?
Lawman (*equally taken aback*) Well ma'am. You just gave it to us on the form you filled out outside and it was brought in to me.
Miss Nelson (*realizing her stupidity*) It's still very clever.
Lawman Ahem. Yes. Now it also says on this form that you wished to talk to someone about a missing person. Is that correct?
Miss Nelson Yes it is.
Lawman Good. I do think we're getting somewhere. Now, if you want us to help we'd better have a few details to help us track down this missing person. (*He selects a form and begins to write*) Let's start at the beginning. Name?
Miss Nelson Nelson.
Lawman (*writing*) Nel ... son. I see that that's the same name you've written on the form outside. Are you related?
Miss Nelson (*giggling*) Oh very good Sergeant Lawman. Very droll!
Lawman (*looking curiously at Miss Nelson and not knowing what on earth she is talking about*) Yes. (*He looks up and says quite loudly*) Sex.

Miss Nelson spins round in her chair, looks behind her then turns back

Miss Nelson Oh I'm sorry. I thought your colleague had come in.
Lawman Colleague? What colleague?
Miss Nelson Mr Blake. Sexton ... Sex for short.
Lawman (*getting impatient*) No! Sex, as in male or female ... as in ... oh you know what I mean ... (*loudly*) sex, sex, sex. (*He realizes he has lost his temper and tries to calm himself*)
Miss Nelson Sergeant Lawman. Honestly. (*Making herself look as feminine as possible*) I would have thought that you could have worked that one out for yourself.
Lawman (*trying to control himself*) I'm afraid I'm not allowed to use guesswork for this job. Now if you'll only answer the questions, no matter how trivial or strange they seem to you, we'll be through a whole lot quicker.
Miss Nelson Female.
Lawman Good. (*Writing*) A short description please.
Miss Nelson Well. (*She proceeds to give a description of herself*) Brown hair; about seven and a half stone ... five foot two ... (*jokingly*) eyes of blue!
Lawman Age?
Miss Nelson Fift——forty-nine.
Lawman Have you a photograph that we could see?
Miss Nelson (*thinking*) A photograph ... No, I don't think ... wait a minute. (*She opens her handbag and fumbles about*) Yes I have! (*She looks at it*) It's not a very good one ... (*she hands it to Lawman*) ... but here it is anyway. Mind you I don't know how this can help you.
Lawman Please let me be the judge of that. (*He takes the photo*) You see there are various things we can do with this photograph. Firstly, we can circulate it through the——(*He looks at it*) Miss Nelson. This appears to be a photograph of yourself.

Miss Nelson Yes that's right Sergeant. Who did you expect it to be, Sophia Loren?
Lawman (*looking at the form that he has filled out*) And I suppose that you are forty-nine, are seven and a half stone; and five feet two inches tall and have eyes of . . . ahem . . . blue eyes.
Miss Nelson Yes of course.

Lawman screws up the piece of paper and throws it in the bin. He picks up his pen

Lawman You came in enquiring about a missing person, Miss Nelson. (*Each word said clearly and precisely*) What is the name of the missing person whom you wish us to try and find?
Miss Nelson Edward . . . Edward Bayes Warrington Smith. He was a direct descendant of the Bayes Warrington who fought with Nelson at Trafalgar.
Lawman Oh. Thank you very much. That little fact will make it a doddle to find him. Date last seen?
Miss Nelson August eleventh . . . nineteen forty-three.
Lawman (*writing*) Aug . . . ust . . . elev . . . enth, nine-teen——(*He looks up*) Haven't you been a little lax in reporting this disappearance, ma'am?
Miss Nelson Yes I suppose I have. But you see I kept on believing that any day I'd see him or hear from him. You see we had this understanding that after the war was over we'd wait for each other at a certain place. We chose the ballroom where we first met, just outside the main doors.
Lawman Go on.
Miss Nelson Well, come VE-Day, I took up my post every night and started to wait. Unfortunately, after the war, they pulled the old ballroom down, and opened a new one on the other side of town. So I had this dilemma. Would Edward wait for me outside the rubble of the old building, or outside the main doors of the new. So I decided to spend the first part of the evening in the rubble and the second part outside the new. Then, they built the new shopping arcade where the old building used to be, and I had to keep running round the shops in case he was waiting in one part, and I was in another. (*After a pause*) Mr Lawman, I've had the feeling lately that something has gone wrong with our arrangement.
Lawman Yes ma'am. I tend to agree with you. Have you by any chance got a photograph of *him*?
Miss Nelson Oh yes of course! (*She takes a photo out of her bag*) This is the last picture we had taken together. (*She starts to sob a little*) I'm sorry. It's just been a bit of a sudden shock to realize . . . to realize he may not be coming back. (*She composes herself and hands the photo to Lawman*) He's in his army uniform . . . I'd just ironed his trousers.
Lawman Look ma'am. We'll do our very best to help. But please don't hold out too much hope.
Miss Nelson Oh Sergeant Lawman. That's something you can't stop me doing. (*She gets up and makes her way to the door*)
Lawman We'll be in touch then.
Miss Nelson Yes. Thank you so much.

Act I, Scene 3

Miss Nelson goes out of the door. Lawman walks over to this desk and picks up the notes he has made. He places them on his desk as the music to Song 4 begins. He sings

Song 4: Funny Lady

Lawman Funny lady, I don't know what to think
Funny lady, feel like I need a drink,
Funny lady.
A lady who just thinks she's missed the boat

(Let me see now what I wrote)

Funny creature, who would ever have guessed
She's a teacher, guess the school's the best place
I should reach her,
In case I find out anything of note.

What a funny life she's had now
It's no wonder that she's sad now,
And I really would be glad now, to help her if I can

(I'm a man with a)

Funny notion, I won't simply just go through
The motion, but I'll tackle this job with devotion
I'll do everything it's possible to do.
Funny lady I've a funny feeling 'bout you.

Outside Lawman's office Miss Nelson takes her compact out of her bag and, looking into the mirror, sings

Miss Nelson Funny lady, take a look at yourself,
Funny lady, you've been left on the shelf
Funny lady, you've got to get yourself out of this mess

Yes, this sacrifice you're making,
No-one's asked you to be taking
And it's your heart that you're breaking all the time

I'm just lonely, all my life no-one really has known me
I wish even that policeman would phone me
But even then, where would it all lead to
(But) funny lady, I've a funny feeling 'bout you.

The Lights fade

Scene 4

Miss Betterby's office

Miss Betterby Mr Duff. I don't have to tell you how much the school apprecia——
Mr Duff (*taking her hand across the desk*) Please! Call me John. We've known each other so long now that I feel we can at least be on first name terms. And may I call you Joan?
Miss Betterby I'd rather you called me June ... my right name.
Mr Duff Oh course of course!
Miss Betterby (*taking a deep breath*) Mr Duff ... John. You do know how very much we appreciate you coming here every year and how tremendously interesting we find your talks—and let me reassure you once again that the girls do not fall asleep but simply close their eyes in order to be able to concentrate better. However, I was just wondering whether this year we could make the lecture a little more ... eh ... a little more stimulating.
Mr Duff I like to be frank——
Miss Betterby You said you were John!
Mr Duff No no no no ... I mean I like to be frank ... straight-forward you know, and I was going to say that I wanted you to be too, Jane.
Miss Betterby June. Look John. We find it simply fascinating hearing about the way that paying-in slips should be filled out and simply thrilling learning about how the bank can assist its customers in making out their last will and testament, but isn't there some other aspect of high finance that can enable the girls to enter into the spirit of things a little more?
Mr Duff I think I know what you're trying to say, Jean.
Miss Betterby June ... but it doesn't matter.
Mr Duff I'm earnest.
Miss Betterby What!
Mr Duff No, I mean that I'm earnest about what I'm going to say. (*After a pause*) Look, I know that what's interesting and fascinating for men, isn't always interesting for the female sex. What do girls want to worry themselves about high finance for anyway? To them I suppose it could almost be ... (*disbelievingly*) boring!
Miss Betterby He's got it. He's got it. By George I think he's got it!
Mr Duff George?

Miss Betterby looks at him for a moment but cannot speak. She makes a gesture at him to forget it!

Stocks!
Miss Betterby (*quite shocked*) Mr Duff. I don't think I've ever heard you use bad language ...
Mr Duff No no no ... stocks ... stocks and shares. That's what I'll talk to them about. (*Getting excited*) We've just brought in a new man, George

Act I, Scene 4 15

Everett's his name, to handle the extra work because we're extending our stocks and shares department. Now *that's* the kind of thing that will excite them isn't it? You see I'm Jack of all trades really.
Miss Betterby Yes Jack! (*Sarcastically*) I'm sure they won't be able to contain themselves.
Mr Duff Good. Now to celebrate the enormous success that I'm sure my talk is going to be, how about you and I having dinner together tomorrow night. I've found this great place in the High Road that does a great Steak Diane ...
Miss Betterby (*almost aside*) June!
Mr Duff (*ignoring her aside*) and three course meal with wine for only five pounds per head. Of course I'd pay for myself!

A long pause during which Miss Betterby looks at him

And leave the tip!
Miss Betterby Look John. One day I'd love to have dinner with you, but at the moment I've got so much on my mind that I just don't feel I'd be very good company. But I *do* thank you for your most genero——(*realizing*)—gen——I do thank you for your offer.
Mr Duff Tell you what then! *King and I!* I can get house seats off one of my customers ... Great stuff! (*Singing*) "Doe a deer, a female deer. Ray a drop ..."
Miss Betterby I think you've got your "does" mixed up. *The King and I* is with Yul Brynner.
Mr Duff Course it is! Silly me! D'you know a lot of people say that if I was to shave the hair off I'd be the spitting image of Yul Brynner. What d'you think? Tell you what. Let's go and see the show and you'll see how much alike we are.
Miss Betterby No thank you, John. Let me get the school's finances off my mind first.
Mr Duff Very well. But I think you're wrong. You know what they say. "All work and no play makes Jack a dull boy" ... Funny thing you know—I always think that should rhyme ... You know ... something like "All work and no play doesn't mean that Jack's gay" ... Oh no! I suppose that wouldn't be right either. Anyway. Point is, that a little bit of fun wouldn't do you any harm. (*He pauses*) However, (*in a different tone*) you bringing up the question of the school finances does lead me to the rather unpleasant subject of the school's bank balance—or more correctly, non-balance! I'm afraid I've had my area office on to me. June, I know your philosophy, but it doesn't seem to go down too well with them when I tell them that "Something will turn up!"
Miss Betterby (*suddenly busying herself and pretending not to hear*) Yes ... em ... how about "Isn't life's natural way?"
Mr Duff Pardon? June what are you talking about?
Miss Betterby "All work and no play isn't life's natural way!" You see, it works nicely ... and it doesn't restrict the gender to male.
Mr Duff June. You wouldn't be trying to change the subject would you?
Miss Betterby Change the—John. Why on earth would I want to do

something like that? Now. Show me your notes on the school talk you're going to give and I'll be pleased to give you my opinion.

Mr Duff (*exasperated*) What's the use! (*He takes some papers out of his brief-case*) "Dear Area Office ... Don't worry! Something will turn up. Yours sincerely, J. Duff. Manager." (*He pauses*) "Dear Mr Duff ... Thank you for your letter. We truly hope that something does turn up ... for you! Like a new job ... 'cos you certainly haven't got one with the bank anymore! Yours sincerely, Area Office."

Miss Betterby (*taking the notes; exaggeratedly*) Thank you John.

We return to this scene in a few minutes but our attention is turned to some girls who have started to listen outside the door of Miss Betterby's study

Cathy Honestly! It's hard to believe isn't it? Two grown adults, who quite evidently like each other, but when it comes to it ...

Gill I know. It's crazy. If I was her I'd have him walking down the aisle already—with handcuffs on!

Susie As it happens, I don't think she's half good enough for him!

Cathy Now we all know why she's saying that don't we? Look Susie. Forget your own heartfelt feelings at the moment and even you would be the first to own up that they'd be very good for each other.

The music for Song 5 begins

They like the same things; share the same views ... I think they're made for each other. It's just that they don't ... don't seem capable of ...

Song 5: Getting It Together

(*Singing*)	Getting it together,
	Getting it to get together
	Getting something moving from the start
	He thinks that he's Yul Brynner
	Says "Let's go halves on dinner"
	That's not the way to win a lady's heart
Susie	They have trouble in ...
	Getting it all going
	I'm afraid her age is showing
	No, she'll never hook a man this way.
	They're like birds of a feather
	And I just don't know whether,
	They'll get it all together come what may,
	Maybe they'll get it all together ... today.

The girls shrug and slowly walk off

The refrain is taken up by Duff, who stands up and sings aside ...

Mr Duff	I have trouble in ...
	Getting it together
	Getting it to get together,
	I don't know what's wrong with me these days.

Act I, Scene 5

    Have I lost my touch now,
    Or asking far too much now?
    OK she won't go Dutch now, that's OK.

    What's it take to start ...
    Getting it all going,
    Quick, my confidence is growing,
    I must just confront her suddenly
    She thinks I'm pretty clever
    But I don't think I'll ever
    Get it all together now you see ...
    I'm waiting for her, to get it together
    With me.

Miss Betterby (*handing him the papers*) Yes. If you add the idea of the Stock Market to this, it will be fine. But John ...
Mr Duff Yes?
Miss Betterby I'll take you up on that offer of dinner, on one conditions.
Mr Duff What's that?
Miss Betterby We split the tip down the middle!

The Lights fade

SCENE 5

The teachers' common room

Two chairs face the stage. In one sits Miss Olden, fast asleep. The other is empty

Madame Souflee enters. She sees Miss Olden sitting in the chair but doesn't realize she is asleep

Madame Souflee Hello Grace. Cup of tea? (*After a pause; more loudly*) I said, "Would you like a cup of tea?"
Miss Olden (*waking with a fright*) Er ... err. Page thirty-two and stop the noise! (*Realizing*) Oh dear! Oh dear!
Madame Souflee Oh I'm sorry, Grace. I didn't realize you were resting.
Miss Olden "Resting"! It's a funny thing isn't it? When you're young they call it "sleeping". When you get to my age they call it "resting".

Madame Souflee smiles

    I suppose the next step is "at rest"! ... I think I'll stick to "resting".
Madame Souflee Oh Grace! You've got a long long time before that step.
Miss Olden Can I have that in writing and with a ten-year guarantee?
Madame Souflee Yes you can! (*Slightly more serious*) Grace, I was thinking the other day. How long have you been at this school?
Miss Olden Well, despite rumours that when they built the school in eighteen seventy-nine they put up the building around me, I've actually

only been here forty-nine years ... well it will be fifty in January. (*She looks round*) Fifty years!
Madame Souflee It's a long time.
Miss Olden A long time? It's forever! And you know the funny thing?
Madame Souflee What's that?
Miss Olden It's only a temporary job!

Madame Souflee laughs

No. I'm serious. I left college and my first teaching job was going to be in Somerset, but it didn't start till the summer term so I came here just to fill in.
Madame Souflee And you stayed.
Miss Olden Well I'll tell you exactly what happened. I was given the new girls in the first form. I can remember some of them even now. Some were shy, some were rather naughty, some were bright and some were ... slow. But I seemed to get very attached to all of them, and they used to come to me with their problems. Not only school problems, but everything.
Madame Souflee They still do!
Miss Olden Well, I remember thinking to myself, "I'll just stay on another term here, to make sure the girls settle in to their second year all right." And then of course I had to see them into the Senior school ... and then I wanted to be with them through their exams ... and of course all the time there were new girls coming into the school ... and I had to watch over them as well ... and the next thing that I knew it was forty-nine years later!
Madame Souflee And are you sorry?
Miss Olden Sorry! How can I be sorry? I've had a wonderful life. You know, years ago I met someone from college that I hadn't seen for donkeys' years. We got chatting and he said to me "How many children have you got?" and quite without thinking I said "five hundred and thirty-two—with two on the way!" Well ... you should have seen his face. But that's the way I think of them you see ... *my* children!
Madame Souflee But Grace. Don't you think you've done enough now? Thousands of girls that have been through this school come back ... year after year ... I've seen it myself. They don't come to see the assembly hall or their classrooms—or even the headmistress! No! They come to see you. Now don't you deserve a well-earned rest?
Miss Olden There you go with that word "rest" again! What you really mean is "Isn't it about time that an old woman like me retired and let the younger ones get on with it?"
Madame Souflee No! That's not what I mean at all! Grace, I know you haven't taken a holiday for years. You've got your brother and sister in Canada who you're always talking about visiting. Surely, *now's* the time?
Miss Olden Time? ... Time. Yes that's the important word. Who knows how much time I've got. If only someone could say to me "You've got three years, four months and nine days left" ... then fine! I'd be able to plan accordingly, but ... (*jokingly*) ... how do I look? Do you think I'll last out the term?

Act I, Scene 5   19

Madame Souflee You look to me as though you'll see the school out ... let alone the term!
Miss Olden That may not be so long! You may be joking, but it's a big worry to me. (*She sees the portrait*) I knew Edwina Roach you know. Wonderful woman. Strict, but very kind and absolutely devoted to the girls. I was just a young thing then ... hard to imagine isn't it?
Madame Souflee Oh stop it!
Miss Olden Well anyway. For some reason or other she took a shine to me. Taught me an awful lot of things about teaching that with all your "streaming" and "television" and modern teaching methods, still seemed to send out nicer and cleverer girls into the world. But she became very ill. She knew she was dying and she chose me ... why I'll never know ... she chose me to promise her that I'd look after the school ... her school. To keep a watch that her girls were happy and that standards didn't fall.
Madame Souflee (*nodding her head slowly in understanding*) And that's why it's so hard for you to leave at the moment. With the school's financial problems being the way they are.
Miss Olden I suppose so. But you know, we've hit rough patches before, and the funny thing is that you only need *one* good year's results for university and suddenly you haven't got enough places at the school to take all the applicants.
Madame Souflee Well, now I understand your problem, Grace. I don't know what I'd do in your position.
Miss Olden Oh, some nights I lie in bed "resting" ... and thinking "Shall I stay? ... Shall I leave? ... Shall I stay ... Shall I leave?" (*She pauses*) You know what I call it?

The music for Song 6 begins

Song 6: Going Round In Circles

(*Singing*) I'm going round in circles
The days are spinning past
Just going round in circles
But getting nowhere fast.

So much I've left undone still
Perhaps so little time
So many miles to run still
So many hills to climb

Mustn't put off till tomorrow
What I should really do today
The problem with tomorrows
They seem to go away

And I'm left with only mem'ries
Some good and yet sublime
But those crazy little circles
They get smaller all the time

> I won't put off till tomorrow
> What I know I should do today
> The problem with tomorrows
> They seem so far away
>
> I'm not getting any younger
> I know that I'm way past my prime
> And those frightening little circles
> They get smaller all the time.

The Lights fade

Scene 6

The school hall

John Duff is concluding his talk to the school

Mr Duff ...And so that, in a nutshell... and a pretty small nutshell, is how the Stock Exchange works. And that's the way that some very rich men have made a lot of their money, and the way that some very poor men have lost it! (*He laughs at his own joke*) Right! Now I'm sure that this year you've got lots and lots of questions to ask me, so let me warn you that I've got to be back at the bank to close up in a couple of hours. So let's get right on with the questions.

There is absolute silence for quite a few seconds

(*A little agitated*) Right! I am now ready for your questions. But one at a time please.

There is still absolute silence

Miss Nelson (*joining Duff on the rostrum and clapping her hands loudly*) Girls! Girls! Wake up! (*She realizes her faux pas*) I mean, "Come alive!" (*Severely*) Now those of you that haven't got any questions for Mr. Duff can come along to classroom five-B where I can set *lots* of history homework.

Every hand goes up with a question. Duff, delighted, puts his hand out to Jessica

Jessica (*turning a little to Miss Nelson*) You see, Miss Nelson, all the questions that kept flooding into my mind whilst Mr Duff was speaking seemed to be answered as he went along. It was really a terribly informative and well-explained lecture and I'm sure all the girls agree with me that it's left us completely... numb!

The girls all nod in agreement

Mr Duff (*to Miss Nelson*) This *has* happened to me a few times before, and is I think quite understandable.

Act I, Scene 6   21

Jessica There *is* however just one small question I would like to ask.
Mr Duff Yes. I'm sure I must have left one or two little holes that need filling.
Jessica Well, towards the end of the lecture you mentioned that some men make a lot of money in the Stock Market and other men lose fortunes.
Mr Duff That's right.
Jessica Well, aren't women allowed to buy shares?
Mr Duff Ha ha ha. Yes. I suppose that's the kind of question I would get from an all girls' school. (*He laughs to himself at his little joke*) But seriously ... I think ... and a lot of people tend to agree with me, that finance is really a bit of a man's world. Of course women *are* allowed to buy and sell shares, and the bank does have the odd elderly lady who wishes to have a dabble now and then, but generally speaking the world of the Stock Market—and indeed all high finance, seems to belong to the male species.

Gill raises her hand. Duff points at her to stand up and speak

Gill So why have you chosen to speak to us today—an all-girls' school?
Mr Duff (*in some difficulty*) Well, most of you will get married and be interested in your husbands' careers; and if they should want to discuss things with you, it's always nice to understand what they're talking about. But let me ask you a question. Do you think you'd do well investing in the Stock Exchange?
School Yes!
Mr Duff That's what I thought you'd say. Good, well let's see shall we! I've worked out a little exercise with Miss Betterby that we thought may interest you. Each individual form is going to be allotted a hypothetical one hundred pounds. Each form will be able to buy and sell shares and at the end of the term the winning form—that is, the form that has lost the least—(*realizing*)—or made the most profit will have a special prize.

The girls clap and chatter excitedly

I was thinking of something like a day at the bank, but I'll leave it to your form teachers to work out the details. Anyway, good luck to you all—I think you may need it!

The girls clap again—this time politely

Duff leaves the hall together with most of the girls

A few girls from 6C remain

Jessica Honestly! The nerve of the man. (*Sarcastically*) "Most of you will get married and be interested in your husbands' careers"—we'll show him what we think of our husbands' careers!
Gill Jessica. I can see wicked thoughts spinning round in your brain.
Jessica Well, I've just had about enough of Mr John Duff! I have got a plan, which I think will show him once and for all which is the clever sex. Are you with me?
Cathy Let's hear it, Jess.

Jessica Well, we're going to play his silly little game: but not just with an imaginary hundred pounds. Oh no! We're going to raid our post office books, and our pocket money and our lunch monies if necessary—and we're going to get together a real one hundred pounds, and then ... then we're going to buy and sell stocks and shares and when we've made a big fat profit we're going to go to Mr Duff and stick it ...
Gill (*excitedly*) Yes?
Jessica Stick it on deposit at ten and a quarter per cent!
Helen May I say something?
Girls (*in bored voices*) No!
Susie It's a super idea Jess, but how are we going to buy the real stocks and shares. None of us exactly has our own personal stock-broker!
Jessica *That* is the stroke of genius that has resulted in your electing me for the third year in succession as your form captain, and why I like to see you grovelling every morning when I come in the room! We're going to buy the shares through the bank.
Cathy Through the bank? But how?
Jessica Come over to the telephone with me and you shall hear. Who's got five p? I promise you'll get it back with interest.

One of the girls hands Jessica a coin. They walk over to a pay telephone whilst Jessica continues

> Luckily, my mother has an account at Duff's bank, and luckily I am able to impersonate my mother to a "t". (*She looks at her watch*) He should be back by now. The bank's only down the road. (*She picks up the phone and dials. She puts on special voice*) Oh hello—Mr Duff please. (*After a pause*) Oh hello Mr Duff, it's Joanna Lang, Jessica's mother. How are you? ... Oh—just this minute come back from the school? ... Oh you must be exhausted you poor thing—those silly girls can be so tiresome! (*She grimaces to the girls*) ... No—it's not an ideal way to spend a Friday is it? ... How can you be of help? Well I'll tell you Mr Duff. I feel that I've reached the age where I'd like to have a little dabble. ... No, a dabble Mr Duff. Yes, that's right . ... On the Stock Market. ... Oh, only about a hundred pounds. ... (*Over-acting*) Oh! What a coincidence. ... Well I hope I do better than they're going to do! ... Well I'd like to open a completely new account for these transactions—called—called ... T.D.A.L. Good ... Well what I'll do is get my little girl Jessica. ... Oh! You met her today. ... Yes sweety isn't she? ... Well I'll get her to drop it into the bank on Monday. Rightio. ... Fine. ... (*Repeating what Duff is saying to her*) Then all I have to do is telephone your new man, Mr Everett every time I want to buy and sell, and I can do that over the phone. ... Lovely! Mr Duff, I just can't tell you how helpful you've been! Goodbye. (*She slowly puts down the phone and sticks her tongue out at it. Then she turns in delight to the others*) Well?

Helen Fantastic!
Cathy Incredible!
Susie Great, Jess! But what does T.D.A.L. stand for, for heaven's sake?
Jessica Teach Duff A Lesson!

Act I, Scene 6   23

The girls roar with laughter

Gill You *were* marvellous Jess, but I'm afraid that as clver as your little ruse is, we're going to look idiots—and *feel* idiots when we've lost the hundred pounds. What do we know about the Stock Market? And to be absolutely honest with you I'm not exactly overboard about the idea of chipping in money that I'm certain to lose.
Helen May I say something?
Girls (*together*) No!
Jessica OK. Gill's asked a good question. Let me answer it by asking you a question, Gill. What does your father do?
Gill (*taken by surprise*) My father ... why he's a Director of Allied Steel.
Jessica How about your father, Helen?
Helen Oh come on, Jess! You know what my father does. He's a Director of Amalgamated Trust.
Jessica Yes, I know Hel, but I want everyone else to know. Don't you see, a lot of the girls' fathers are Directors of Public Companies. We all hear them talking business on the phone, or chatting things over with our mothers—we've just never really taken any interest in what they've been saying—UP TO NOW!
Susie Well that's OK. for Gill and Helen and a few of the other girls. But my father runs a fishmonger's in the High Street; Debbie's dad's a GPO engineer ... and so on. How can we help?
Jessica Three weeks ago we sent Carole Ashcroft to Coventry for owning up to Miss Nelson that we all copied her history homework. Right?
Helen Quite right! Rotten sneak. (*After a pause*) What's that got to do with anything?
Jessica We are all going to apologize to Miss Ashcroft; Tell her she did the right thing and that we all want to be friends.
Gill What! Are you kidding? What on earth for?
Jessica Because her father is a stockbroker.

The girls are silent for a few moments

Now we're going to ask Miss Ashcroft to help us with our little ploy by taking an enormous interest in her father's profession and because she'll be so delighted that we're all talking to her again, I've got a feeling she'll co-operate. Susie, your job is to get together with Debbie and all the other girls and to learn all about stocks and shares. Pretend you've got a GCE coming up on it in a week's time! We'll give you all the information, and it's up to your team to tell us what we should buy and sell.
Cathy It's brilliant. I've got to admit it. Brilliant. You know what I like about it?

The music for Song 7 begins

Song 7: It's Easy

Cathy   It's easy, it's easy. It really is so easy,
Gill   When she came up with this idea I thought that she'd gone mad

Susie	It's simple. So simple. It's really very simple
Gill	Now I think it's the best idea that she has ever had.

The girls produce the Financial Times *and other newspapers which they hold up and read*

Helen	ICI
Cathy	Two six two
Jessica	Must buy them today.
Gill	GEC
Susie	Buy a few. Merger on the way
Helen	Nettlewood
Cathy	They're no good. Profit's very small
Jessica	United Bread.
Gill	My daddy said their shares were gonna fall.
All	It's easy, it's easy
Helen	It's devilishly easy
Cathy	I know within a month or two we'll all be millionaires.
Gill	It's simple, so simple, it's really much too simple
Jessica	Who'd ever think we'd have such fun with boring stocks and shares.
Helen	Marks and Spencer
Cathy	One one eight
Jessica	They've got a lot of stock
Gill	Polly Peck
Susie	I'll just check ... steady as a rock.
Helen	De La Rue
Cathy	Divi due, think we should invest
Susie	Beckham Ross
Jessica	My dad's the boss. He really needs a rest.
All	It's easy, it's easy
Helen	It really is too easy
Cathy	Mr Duff is gonna have a big surprise in store
Gill	It's simple, it's simple can you believe how simple Jessica you don't think that we're breaking any law?
Jessica	NAAAAAAAAAH! It's easy, it's easy. Now don't be such a bore.

CURTAIN

ACT II

Scene 1

Outside the ballroom. We hear music coming from inside

Miss Nelson is standing alone ... waiting

Sergeant Lawman approaches

Lawman Why! Good-evening Miss Nelson.
Miss Nelson Sergeant Lawman! What are you doing in this part of the world?
Lawman (*ignoring the question*) So you really do come up here every evening?
Miss Nelson Yes of course! I told you I did. Once I've made an arrangement with someone—as I did with Edward—I don't easily break it. Besides, I have this fear that the one evening I didn't come would be the one evening that Edward chose to see if I'd remembered. But tell me! Have you any news of him for me?
Lawman Unfortunately not, ma'am. But I must say I do respect your absolute devotion to this duty. Don't see a lot of it today. Blimey! I know a fellow who popped out the house for some cigarettes and his wife sued him for desertion!

They both laugh

Miss Nelson So why *are* you here, Inspector? I don't think this is your regular beat ... I haven't seen you come this way in thirty years.
Lawman (*laughing*) No. You're right. It's not. I don't know ... Yes I do. To be absolutely honest I think I wanted to see for myself it was true ... about you waiting every night for him. I must say, it shows tremendous character.
Miss Nelson No it doesn't, Inspector. I'm not a fool—at least not that big a fool. I know that all it shows is what a pathetic love-sick female I've been all these years. I know that whilst I've been standing here watching life pass me by—well, life has passed me by! I realized that years ago, but even by the time I realized it, it was too late. I'm sure I don't have to tell you, Inspector, that maybe only once in a lifetime does Mister—or Miss—Right come along. And when he came—well, I just couldn't let him go that easily could I?
Lawman I know what you mean all right, miss. D'you know? I'm going to tell you something that I've never told another soul! When I started out in the Force, I was dating this lovely girl. She wanted us to settle down and have a family. That was fine ... just what I wanted too. The only thing

was, she couldn't stand the fact that I was a copper. Couldn't bear the thought of the front doorbell going and someone telling her that I'd been hurt—or worse. Her slogan was "Let the Force be without you"!

Miss Nelson So?

Lawman So, she asked me to make a choice. I never could. Julie or the Force. I loved them both. So one day, she was gone, and ever since I've wondered whether that was the biggest mistake I've every made in my life ... but it probably wasn't! 'Cos I've made a few since then!

The music for Song 8 begins

Miss Nelson Oh! We all make mistakes ... it's part of life.

Lawman Course we do. Why I remember ...

Song 8: We All Make Mistakes

(*Singing*) One night I drove home in my car I passed the local cinema
And saw this kinda torchlight in the air
I thought it looked suspicious so
I broke in round the back you know
I thought I'd give those villains quite a scare.

I broke the office door down with my foot—but goodness me!
The manager was in there with his girl-friend on his knee.

(*Speaking*) So I said to 'em ... "Good-evening sir" ... "Nice night isn't it?" "Though it looks a bit like rain" ... "Pardon the intrusion but ..."

(*Singing*) We all make mistakes and we try to forget 'em
Of course those mistakes get us down if we let 'em
We all make mistakes but the ones that I make are the best.

Miss Nelson One night as I was standing here, I saw this man in black appear
I knew it was my Edward come for me.
My heart was beating oh so fast, and just as he was walking past
I grabbed his hand so very lovingly.
"I'm here! I'm here!" I shouted, "This is where we said we'd meet"
I spent the night in prison for accosting on the street!

(*Speaking*) I told the judge ... I was very very sorry ... It would never happen again ... I said "Please understand".

(*Singing*) We all make mistakes that are so hard to live with,
If we'd only thought it right out to begin with
We all make mistakes but the ones that I make are the best.

Lawman We had this tip-off, there would be a robbery at number three

I volunteered to lay in wait and hide.
The plan was, when I heard them come, I'd blow my whistle
And they'd run into the cold arms of the Law outside.

The only problem was you see I didn't hear a peep,
I always take a sleeping pill, and so I fell asleep.

(*Speaking*) But I told the sergeant on duty ... "One of those things sir ..." "Won't happen again sir" ... "You have my word on it ... but ..."
(*Singing*) We all make mistakes and we try to forget 'em
Miss Nelson Of course those mistakes get us down if we let them
Both We all make mistakes but the ones that I make are the best.
We all make mistakes but the ones that we make are the best.
Lawman Look Miss Nelson. It's getting a bit late now. Chances are he won't turn up tonight. What d'you say you and I get a bite to eat. I'm off duty now, and quite honestly ... I could do with the company.
Miss Nelson Do you know, I think that's a lovely idea.

She takes his arm and they walk off together. Suddenly she stops and looks at him

I've always wanted to have a police escort!

They walk off

The Lights fade

Scene 2

The Classroom of 6C. It is two months later

The girls are seen to be pouring over copies of financial papers. On the blackboard is a graph of share movements and the F.T. Index. Susie is standing at the door on look-out. One of the girls goes over to the blackboard and writes the date

Susie There's someone coming!

The girls immediately start to put the papers away and clean the blackboard

OK hold it. It's only Jessica.

The girls moan with relief

Jessica walks in looking extremely depressed

Cathy Hi Jess! What's the matter with you. You look as though there's been another Wall Street Crash!
Jessica I s'pose there has been in a way. It's certainly black Monday

anyway! (*She slumps into a chair*) I received the weekly bank statement in the post this morning on the T.D.A.L. account.

Gill Gosh! It's lucky you always get to them first, Jess!

Jessica Lucky! (*Even louder*) Lucky! I'm up all blooming night, scared to go to sleep in case I miss the postman in the morning and she calls it lucky! I call it jolly UNlucky actually!

Gill Sorry, Jess, I never realized the sacrifices you have to make in the line of duty.

Jessica Actually, my parents are terribly confused by the whole thing. Here I am, every Monday morning, washed, dressed and ready and eager to go to school at six o'clock in the morning, and the rest of the week wild elephants can't get me out of bed!

The girls laugh

Susie (*impatiently*) Well! What does the statement say? We've been doing fantastically haven't we?

Jessica (*miserably*) Oh yes. We've been doing fantastically all right. (*She proceeds to open the bank statement and reads aloud*) Ladies! We show a credit balance of... three thousand, four hundred and twenty-six pounds and eleven pence.

The girls all scream and cheer. Jessica continues to sit there depressed

Cathy So why the long face, Jessica? This is fantastic! And we've done exactly the same shares with our imaginary hundred pounds in the school competition, so we're bound to have won first prize in that as well!

Helen (*sarcastically enthusiastic*) A day at the bank! Gosh. I can't wait!

Jessica Look you dummies. Great! Fantastic! Now what?

Helen What do you mean?

Jessica Exactly what I say. Now what? What do we do with the money. What do we do with this wonderful three thousand four hundred and twenty-six pounds... and eleven pence?

Cathy (*shrugging*) Well, how about if we... SPEND IT!

Shouts of "Yes" and "Absolutely" from the other girls

Gill Yeh. I'm pretty sure I could get through that money quite easily on my own—let alone have to share it with twenty-four of you other spend-thrifts!

Everyone laughs but Jessica is still not amused

Jessica (*impatiently*) Fine! You'll spend it. How are you going to get it?

Gill How am I going to get... I'll go down to the bank... (*She stops to think for just a second*)... or you'll go down to the bank and you'll write ... (*she slows down alarmingly*) ... out a ... oooooohhhaaaaaaaaaaahhh!

Jessica I think Gill has got the point! If I was just to go down to the bank and ask for three thousand pounds of my mother's money to be handed over to me, I've got a slight hunch that even Mr honest-and-trusting Duff, *might* just want to phone my mother to check that it's all right ... that's if I was prepared to forge my mother's signature on the cheque in the first place!

Act II, Scene 2   29

Helen Oh Jessica! This is rotten. What are we going to do?
Jessica Well it was nearly a whole lot worse. I also intercepted this note from Mr Duff to my mother. (*She gets out the note and reads*) "Dear Mrs Lang, Hearty congratulations on your little dabble. I feel a celebration lunch is called for, courtesy of the bank! Please telephone me so we can arrange it. Yours very truly, John Duff."
Gill (*same noise as before*) Oooooohhhaaaaaaaaaahhh!
Jessica Before Gill continues with her Tarzan impersonations, let me inform you that I have in fact dealt with that problem.
Helen How?
Jessica The same way we bought the shares! I phoned up old Duff—pretending to be my mother and told him that I was terribly busy at the moment, putting the final touches to my latest novel, and so, as much as I appreciated the offer, I'd like to take a raincheck.
Susie Oh well done Jess, but I didn't know your mother wrote novels?
Jessica No, neither does she. But we seemed to have built up this image of my mother in Duff's eyes of a brilliant financial wizard, and I thought it kind of kept up the illusion. Anyway, he was terribly impressed.
Gill So! what's the answer to our problem Jessica?
Jessica I'm afraid there is only one answer.
Helen What's that?
Jessica We've got to *lose* the money!

The girls all cry "What?" in horrified chorus

That's right. I'm afraid that I've been wrestling with the problem all morning and it is the only answer. You see, we can't spend it; we can't just leave it where it is, accumulating interest because one day my mother would find out she's three thousand pounds richer, and we certainly can't own up about it ... so I'm afraid the only answer is ... we've got to lose it.
Cathy Jessica. You said just now that we can't own up about it. Are you sure that isn't the best answer?
Jessica Well, perhaps the best person to answer that question is our legal expert Gill Thorn. I probably should have told you, but I didn't want to worry you unnecessarily. A few weeks ago, Gill spoke to me because she was very very concerned about something. Go on Gill. You explain it.
Gill Well, as you all know, I'm taking A-level law and a few weeks ago I read something that didn't make me all that happy. You see, basically, we have been committing a variety of legal offences ranging from simple common-or-garden fraud, to "obtaining privileged information concerning a public company and using it for financial gain". Plus a whole lot of other little crimes in-between.
Cathy So what does that all add up to?
Gill About three to five years actually.

The girls are deathly silent

Jessica Which is why, the only answer I'm afraid is to lose all the money.
Susie How stupid!
Jessica Nevertheless that is what we must do.

Helen Can I say something?
Girls NO!
Jessica What we've got to do is pick a share that we're absolutely cretain is going to fall drastically. If we're really lucky the firm will go completely bust! We'll invest the whole three thousand quid, and pray that we lose the lot.
Susie How stupid!
Cathy No, I'm afraid Jessica's right. We've got to do it, and we've got to do it now. Girls! Financial hats on please!

They bring out their papers and start studying

Susie (*screaming*) This is stupid.

The music for Song 9 begins

Song 9: It's Stupid (Reprise of "It's Easy")

Susie	It's stupid, it's stupid. This really is quite stupid
Gill	We've got to lose three thousand pounds and got to lose it quick!
Helen	It's crazy, it's crazy I think we're going crazy
Jessica	All that lovely money—it's enough to make you sick.

Susie (*speaking*) Read 'em out from the top Gill!

Gill APV, Acrow A, Airfix, Lacy Ash,
Beecham, Boots, Bejam Coutts, are we being rash?
Susie (*taking over reading the list out*) Currys' Christies Cadbury,
We're already up to "C"
And I can't find a single share that looks in jeopardy

Cathy	It's stupid it's stupid. Don't like this game it's stupid
Gill	Tryin' to lose a fortune isn't my idea of fun
Helen	It's crazy, real crazy, I don't like actin' crazy
Jessica	And this goes down as the craziest thing that we have ever done.

Helen	IMI
Cathy	Forty-nine dropping very fast,
Jessica	MAM
Gill	No, they're fine. Assets are just vast
Susie	London Brick?
Helen	Need a kick, but they'll be OK
Cathy	I think I've found the very share where dividends won't pay!

It's Stodgy ... P. Stodgy. Its shares are really dodgy
The experts all agree within a week they'll take a fall
Gill (*speaking*) What do they do?
Helen (*speaking*) Who are they?

Act II, Scene 3

Cathy They're under "mining" ... "refining". I think it's perfect timing
Patrick Sergeant says that there's no hope for them at all
All It's stupid, it's crazy. Oh why is life so cruel?

The Lights fade

Scene 3

The school hall

Miss Betterby is standing on the dais addressing the school

Miss Betterby Well girls. Our nineteen eighty-one Drama Festival is nearly at an end ...

Sarcastic "Aaaahs" from the girls

I would like to thank all the teaching staff for their hard work, and in particular the music department. We now have I'm afraid the last item from the school choir ...

More sarcastic "Aaaahs"

Followed by a poem from Gill Thorn called "Mr Examiner".

Mild applause

The school choir walk on stage and sing a rather short four-part piece (see Song 10) Applause from the school

Gill walks on to the stage and recites her piece

The school choir sing softly in the background

Poem/Song 10: Mr Examiner

Gill (*speaking*) We're sitting crouched behind old tables,
Waiting expectantly like lambs,
I'll do as well as I am able
But God I really hate exams.
I tell myself it's so important
I've got myself in such a state.
It would make my parents both so happy
Why's it so hard to concentrate.

The years at school of preparation
I guess they've all been for today
Think of the joy and jubilation,
If only I make out OK
I don't care if I don't get Oxbridge,
I'll leave those silly hopes behind
Give me the chance ... I swear I'll take it
Mr Examiner ... please be kind.

Gill and Chorus My life is really in your hands sir
(*singing*) I hope you know the power you've got
For you could upset all my plans sir,
Or you could help them quite a lot.
The difference 'tween one tick or cross sir,
Can't be too strongly underlined.
Though you don't even know my name sir
Mr Examiner ... please be kind
Mr Examiner ... please be kind.

Applause again from the stage, following which Miss Betterby resumes her position on the dais

Miss Betterby Thank you Gill, that was lovely ... And now, you will be delighted to hear that Mr John Duff has most kindly agreed to come here today to present the prize for the inter-class competition. Girls, please welcome Mr Duff as only you can.

Very, very sparse applause. Susie however claps most enthusiastically and continues clapping after everyone else has stopped. All the other girls look at her

Duff takes his place at the dais next to Miss Betterby who hands him an envelope

Well, Mr Duff, here are the results. I think you may be a little surprised!

Mr Duff Thank you Miss Betterby, I don't think I will be! Ho ho ho! Right. Here are the results that you've been waiting for. I will read them out class by class (*He is quite obviously thoroughly enjoying himself, and looking forward to the bad results he knows will follow*) Class Five-A. Right. Now Five-A I'm afraid lost one hundred and twenty-five pounds. Hard luck, Five-A, lucky we don't have to ask you to put the money in yourselves eh? Now Five-B. Well, they did a bit better. They only lost forty pounds ... Still not exactly the way to make your fortune though eh? Five-C ... good! Good show, they made a profit of ... one pound twenty-five p. Well, it's a start isn't it? Howard Hughes had to start somewhere! Ho ho ho! (*He becomes serious and intent*) But girls, perhaps you see what I meant a few months ago when I said that finance really was a bit of a man's world. Anyway, on with the results. Form Six-A ... oh dear. They really came a cropper. They lost three hundred and twelve pounds. Six-B have lost twelve pounds fifty p ... not bad, Six-B, and lastly, Six-C (*not realizing*) have made a profit of three thousand, four hundred and twenty-six pounds and eleven pence. Good. Now I——(*He stops, looks at the paper*) Miss Betterby, there's been a bit of a mistake made on this slip of paper ...

Miss Betterby joins Duff on stage and talks quietly to him. He becomes more and more visibly shaken. Miss Betterby eventually leaves the dais

(*Unenthusiastically*) I am delighted to tell you that Six-C have won the first prize, with a profit of three thou ... (*he has trouble in saying the*

Act II, Scene 3

words) ... thousand, four hundred and twenty-six pounds and eleven pence.

The school roar with delight

Perhaps the form captain of Six-C would like to come up and receive the prize.

Jessica joins Duff on the dais

I have much pleasure ... and amazement ... in presenting you with this wonderful book, which I am sure the whole class will enjoy reading, entitled *The Thrills of Banking*.

Jessica takes the book and makes the following speech to the tune of the school song. The music for Song 11 begins

Song 11: School Song (Reprise)

Jessica Without your help and guidance, we never would have won.
Our efforts have paid dividends—if you'll excuse the pun.
You've been our inspiration in seeing this job through
'Tis not Six-C should have this prize.
No Mr Duff it's you.

Jessica repeats the above whilst the school sing the counter-melody, below

What a lot of old rot, what a lot of old rot she has to say.
All our efforts are in vain, it's all money down the drain now anyway.
Some inspiration he hasn't got a clue
We nominate the biggest prize
And Mr Duff it's you.

At the end of Jessica's speech the school clap approvingly and file out of the hall

Duff is left in the hall alone, until Susie, who has been watching him from afar, rushes over to him

Susie Oh, Mr Duff ... Mr Duff!
Mr Duff (*turning round and seeing Susie*) Yes? Oh it's Susie isn't it?
Susie (*thrilled*) Oh. You remember my name!
Mr Duff Well, yes Susie. It's difficult to forget because you have written to me every week for the last two years for a job and I think you've sent me nine ... or is it ten ... photographs of yourself so let alone just knowing your name, I really am beginning to think of you as an old friend!
Susie Oh, thank you Mr Duff! But may I have a word with you now?
Mr Duff Susie, if it's about a job in the bank again, I can only tell you the same thing I told you last time we met. The bank's official position is that we're very happy to consider all applications, but you cannot stipulate that you will only work for the bank if it's in my branch!

Susie As it happens Mr Duff, it isn't about a job. I wanted to talk to you about something ... much more serious.
Mr Duff More serious ... more serious than the bank! Well, we'd better hear it ... but I've got a feeling I know what it is?
Susie You do?
Mr Duff Yes. Don't worry. Lots of girls of your age have the same problem.
Susie They do?
Mr Duff Yes of course. And let me put your mind at rest by saying that it's quite all right, and I agree.
Susie You do?
Mr Duff Yes of course. You just tell me what kind of an overdraft you were thinking about.
Susie An overdraft? Mr Duff ... I don't want an overdraft.
Mr Duff You don't, Oh. All right, Well, let's see. You don't want the bank to help you with your will do you?
Susie (*exasperated*) No! Of course I don't want a will. I want to ... Oh you're making this so difficult for me ... I want to talk to you about ... love!
Mr Duff (*shrieking in amazement*) Love! LOVE! What do I know about love? I'm a bank manager ... (*Calming himself down, he now turns aside and recites aloud to himself*) "Rule thirty-one-b. Listen to every problem that a customer—or potential customer, may have. Try to offer unprejudiced and sound advice. *Never* mock or make fun of the most trivial enquiry." (*He turns back to Susie*) Ahem ... of course ... love! What is it exactly that you wished to confer with me about ... about love?
Susie Well, Mr Duff. I think I'm "in" love, with someone ... someone who barely knows that I exist; and right at this very moment I'm trying to pluck up courage to tell him. (*She repeats, to make the point*) Right at this very moment!
Mr Duff (*oblivious*) Well, my child ... (*realizing*) ... young lady have you thought about discussing this with your mother?
Susie Oh, she wouldn't understand. You see the man in question is quite a lot older than I am ... not that he looks it ... or acts it. But he must be, because you have to be a certain age to be a ban——(*realizing*) Ban—bandleader. Yes. That's what he is. A bandleader.
Mr Duff (*puzzled*) Why does that make him old? I thought today quite a lot of bandleaders were young fellows. (*After a pause*) It's not Joe Loss is it? (*He roars with laughter*)
Susie (*near to tears*) I'm delighted to see you think it's so funny Mr Duff. I'm talking to you because I always thought you were a kind, considerate and understanding man, who would listen to me and *not* make fun of me.
Mr Duff (*aside*) "Rule forty-four-d. Never ... never bring a customer—or potential customer, to the point of tears. Ensure that any bad news is sent in a letter so that the customer can cry in the privacy of their own home." Susie! (*Looking back at her*) Of course I was not making fun of you. Would I do that! No ... think of me as your "Listening Banker"! (Ha ha ha).
Susie All right Mr Duff. Let me try and explain.

Act II, Scene 4 35

The music for Song 12 begins

Song 12: I'm In Love, Mr Duff

(*Singing*) I'm in love, Mr Duff, and I've simply had enough,
Love's not easy when you're only seventeen.
Though I've tried hard to hide it
Deep down right inside it really hurts,
Mr Duff, d'you know what I mean?

You see it's tough, Mr Duff, tell me strictly "off the cuff"
What advice have you that I can take heed of?
Would you say "Just ignore it."
"There's no known cure for it"
I'm in love ... Mr Duff.

Duff lights his pipe, then slowly walks off

I won't bluff, Mr Duff, you can just stand there and puff
You can laugh at me, but tell me what to do?
For the truth of the matter,
I'm mad as a hatter over you—yes I'm afraid it's true
'Cos Mr Duff, I'm in love with you.

Susie, who has been looking straight ahead and not at Duff turns to see how he has taken the confession only to find he has left

The Lights fade

SCENE 4

Detective Sergeant Lawman's office

Madame Souflee is seated at the desk opposite Lawman

Lawman Madame Souflee. I'm very grateful to you for coming over here today. As I said to you on the telephone, this is, perhaps a rather "delicate" matter.

Madame Souflee Sergeant Lawman. I am French! I am used to these delicate matters!

Lawman Quite so. Well, I wanted to have a chat with you about Miss Nelson ... I know you and she are good friends.

Madame Souflee Miss Nelson! Don't tell me *she's* done anything wrong?

Lawman Oh no no no! Nothing like that. Look Madame Souflee, this is a bit of a confidential matter—you might say even "personal". But you see, Miss Nelson came to see me a few weeks ago. She wanted the police to try and locate a missing person. A Mr Edward Bayes Warrington Smith. Has she ever mentioned him to you?

Madame Souflee Oh yes of course! For years she has driven me mad about "her Edward". I have often tried to persuade her to come out with me some evenings and have some "ooh la la" but no ... she still waits for Edward to return to her.

Lawman Yes. Well I'm afraid that's the problem. You see Madame Souflee, her Edward is *not* going to return to her. It only took us a few days to find out that an Edward Bayes Warrington Smith got married to a Clara Bagshoot on the twenty-fifty April, nineteen forty-five at All Saints Church, Whitby. I don't think that there's a strong likelihood of there being two gentlemen with that name—but anyway, this one's a descendent of the Bayes Warrington that fought with Nelson so I think we've got the right man.

Madame Souflee What did Mary say when you told her all this?

Lawman Well... that's the point. You see, I haven't told her... I kept on making appointments for her to come into the office so that I could tell her—but each time she came in and I saw her, well... she looked so... "hopeful"... that I never had the heart. So I'd make up some excuse as to why I'd asked her to come in ... I'd ask her some useless bit of information or something.

Madame Souflee I see.

Lawman Well, I'm not quite sure you do ... You see the truth of the matter is that I've grown mighty fond of Mary, and I don't really want to be the one to have to break the news to her and end thirty-five years of hope that she's lived with. On the other hand, if she doesn't learn the truth from someone, then she's gonna continue to live in hope—and that's not going to help my chances.

Madame Souflee And what did you want me to do, Sergeant?

Lawman Well, it may sound to you like a coward's way out, but I was hoping that you—being her good friend—could break the news to her. I know it's asking a lot but——

Madame Souflee Sergeant Lawman... Mary knows!

Lawman What!

Madame Souflee I said "She knows". (*After a pause*) In nineteen forty-five Mary received a letter from Edward. In it, he told her that he had met a girl; fallen very much in love with her—and married her. He said that Mary should forget all about him because what they had shared together had been simply—as he put it—"a wartime fling".

Lawman Blimey!

Madame Souflee Of course I didn't even know Mary then. Her brother told me about it a few years ago. He was in the room when she got the letter. He said she went deathly white, then screwed it up and threw it in the waste-paper basket. He couldn't understand what had shocked her so much, so he retrieved the letter and read it. He tried to talk to her about it, but she denied that she'd ever received a letter and went quite hysterical, calling her brother a liar. After that she became quite ill.

Lawman But haven't you ever mentioned it to her?

Madame Souflee Only once, and the same thing happened. I never mentioned it again.

Lawman I see.

Madame Souflee So what are you going to do, Sergeant? I'm afraid I haven't been of much help.

Lawman On the contrary Madame Souflee. I don't know what I'm going to do, but as a policeman I can tell you, it's always nice to be completely aware of all the information. (*He looks at his watch*) As a matter of fact, she's coming here in a few minutes ... I'd timed it rather well in case you agreed to tell her ... but now, well I'd just better start thinking up one of my "excuses" for asking her down here!

Madame Souflee (*rising*) I hope everything works out well, Sergeant.

Lawman Thank you, Madame. So do I. Perhaps it would be wiser if she didn't know you'd been here. I wonder if you'd mind going out the other door?

Madame Souflee Not at all.

Lawman Thanks. Goodbye.

Madame Souflee Au revoir.

Madame Souflee exits

The music for Song 13 begins. Lawman paces a step or two and then sings

Song 13: Going Round In Circles (Reprise)

Lawman   I'm going round in circles,
The days are spinning past
Just going round in circles
But getting nowhere fast.

Those circles keep revolving
Oh God why don't they go
And tell me what I'm solving
By hesitating so.

Mustn't put off till tomorrow
What I should really do today
Now I must force myself to tell her
I wonder what she'll say.

We're not getting any younger
I know that I'm way past my prime
And those frightening little circles
They get smaller all the time.

Miss Nelson enters

Lawman Mary. It's nice to see you. You look lovely.

Miss Nelson Thank you Harry. You look a bit worried. Anything the matter?

Lawman Oh ... just the normal things you know. Do you know that this town is famous for holding the record for stolen bicycles in England? The latest figures we've got show that an average of seventeen bicycles are stolen every day in this town. I sometimes wonder where all those blooming bikes are! I don't see that many *on* the roads.

Miss Nelson Do you catch many of the thieves?

Lawman Naaa! We'd need to bring in a whole division just to look after bicycle thieves to do the job properly. I once had an idea though. Everyone with a bike should have a licence—same as with a car ... and the bike and the licence should have the same number written on them.

Miss Nelson Harry! That sounds a marvellous idea. What happened?

Lawman I sent it up to the Yard ... but someone put a spoke in it!—Here! ... That's a good one isn't it? Someone put a *spoke* in it! ... Get it? Anyway ... enough about bikes. Let's get back to the business in hand.

Miss Nelson I didn't know we had any business in hand Harry?

Lawman Well, you see Mary. I've got some news about Edward.

Miss Nelson Edward! ... Oh Harry tell me! Just tell me ... is it ... bad news?

Lawman Yes Mary. I'm afraid it is rather bad. But I think you already know.

Miss Nelson Already know? (*After a pause*) Yes ... yes I suppose I do. I always realized deep down that the only reason he wouldn't come back to me was if he was ... (*softer*) dead.

Lawman Dead! ... No Mary he's——

Miss Nelson I did try to find out after the war from the War Office, but there were so many poor soldiers who were killed without knowing their names or——

Lawman Mary! You must listen to me. (*He picks up a piece of paper and reads*) "Mr and Mrs Bayes Warrington Smith——

Miss Nelson Yes ... yes. We would have been married as soon as he returned. That was always the plan. (*Almost to herself*) Mrs Bayes Warrington Smith Nelson! We'd decided to use my last name you know ... how strange that fate had ... (*She sits down unable to speak*)

Lawman Mary, you must listen to me.

Miss Nelson Harry. I've heard all I want to hear. In a way you know I'm pleased to have learned the truth. I've got a funny feeling that the news will make a lot of difference to me ... I mean a lot of difference to my life from now on. Thank you Harry for being so kind and helpful ... all this trouble you've been to. (*She pauses*) Can I ask you one last thing?

Lawman Yes of course.

Miss Nelson How did he die?

Lawman (*after a long pause*) All that we could find out was that he died a hero, giving his own life to save others.

Miss Nelson (*nodding*) Yes ... that's right.

Lawman Mary?

Miss Nelson Yes Harry.

Lawman There is one other thing I wanted to say to you. You remember I told you about the girl I nearly married? The girl who didn't want a copper as a husband?

Miss Nelson Yes of course.

Lawman Well, how would *you* feel about ... about ... taking the Law into your own hands?

Miss Nelson (*stretching out her arms to Lawman*) I think that would be very nice Harry ... very nice indeed.

The Lights fade

Scene 5

The classroom

Gill Am I noivous!
Cathy Oh come on, Gill. You've got nothing to be nervous about. The way you've been swatting and studying these last few months I bet you know more than the examiners.
Helen (*half-aside*) Not difficult!
Jessica Helen's right. From some stories I've heard these examiners are really weird, but you don't have to worry, when they were giving out the brains you seem to have managed to get a double portion.
Gill I don't know what's worse. The exams or the interviews. Before I took the written exams I was sure *they* were, but now . . .
Cathy Just remember to look confident. That way even if you give a wrong answer the chances are that the examiner will think that he's wrong and you're right! Do you think it will be a man or a woman?
Gill Well I'm kinda hoping for a man, then I'll be able to use all my female wiles on him.
Helen I'd pray for a woman if I were you!

Everyone laughs

They are still laughing as Susie enters

Gill Hi Susie, where you been?
Susie (*distressed*) Me? Oh I've just been . . . I went . . . I needed to go . . .
Jessica She's been with John Duff.
Cathy How'd you make out Sue?
Susie He hates me! He thinks I'm immature and stupid. He's horrible and insensitive and I hate him.
Cathy Not too good eh? Never mind. Today we've all got our problems. You've got John Duff, Gill's got a university entrance interview and I've got—(*holding up a book*)—*The Thrills of Banking*!
Jessica (*laughing*) I must say that I thought having to read that book was a pretty stiff punishment that old Betterby set you, just for talking in Assembly. I think I'd rather have had a hundred lines . . . in fact I think I'd rather have a thousand lines! What on earth were you talking about?
Cathy I said one or two rather disrespectful things about Mr Duff I'm afraid.
Jessica No wonder you got into trouble. I understand she and our Mr Duff are a bit of a joint account at the moment.
Gill Talking about our friendly banker, how are our shares doing?
Jessica (*miserably*) Wonderfully I suppose—if you consider losing a fortune wonderful! The account's down to under four hundred pounds—and dropping fast.
Cathy (*gloomily*) Wonderful!
Gill Great!

Helen Fantastic!
Susie Stupid!
Jessica Oh for crying out loud, don't start that again! No. I am the first to admit that the whole episode was an unmitigated disaster.
Cathy That isn't quite true, Jessica. We did get something out of it.
Jessica What's that?
Cathy (*holding up the book*) *The Thrills Of Banking.*

The girls laugh

Gill All right. This is it kids! I gotta go or I'll be late. Wish me luck.
Helen (*standing and slowly walking over to Gill*) Can I say something?

Gill simply shakes her head. As she exits, she passes Madame Souflee who is walking into the classroom

Madame Souflee Bonjour. Bonjour.
Girls *Bonjour* Madame Souflee.
Madame Souflee Aujourd'hui vous avez un leçon pour quarante minutes mais ce n'est pas... (*She continues talking in French but quietly enough for the following dialogue to be heard*)
Jessica (*to the girl next to her*) Do you know, I have this awful nightmare that one day she comes into the classroom nattering away like this, and we're all unconscious before we can understand that she's telling us the school's on fire and we've got to get out quick!
Madame Souflee Jessica. Stand up please.
Jessica (*in amazement*) That's English! You just spoke in English!
Madame Souflee That's right. I wanted to be sure you understood me! You have detention for the next five nights... comprenez-vous?
Jessica (*dejectedly*) Oui.
Madame Souflee Bien. Et maintenant—(*she pauses*)—and now... as I was saying before, as it is such a nice day, I think we can go out to the school fields and have our lesson there.

The girls are evidently happy about this and file out

Jessica is left alone with Madame Souflee

Jessica Madame Souflee, I'm sorry I was talking before, but could I possibly do my detentions next week. You see I'm rehearsing for the school musical each day after school this week.
Madame Souflee Oh yes, I've heard about it... something about girls in a school who buy stocks and shares isn't it?
Jessica Yeh! It's not very good—(*she pauses*)—but it'll earn some money for the school, which needs money just like the school in the play.

This last dialogue really confuses Madame Souflee who tries to work out what Jessica has said. She tries to think it out quietly to herself. She points at Jessica, at the audience, to herself, to the audience again

Madame Souflee Very well. It is a good cause... they are both good causes.
Jessica Oh thank you Madame Souflee. (*After a pause*) May I ask you a question?

Act II, Scene 6   41

Madame Souflee Mais oui.
Jessica There you go again. That's my question actually. Why do you talk to us in French all the time, you speak English so well?
Madame Souflee First of all, because it is better for all of you to hear as much French as possible and second . . . because . . . because I am French. (*She pauses*) Sometimes I am very unhappy about leaving my Paree, and if I speak in my own language it makes me feel that I will be back there soon.
Jessica I never realized that you must get homesick.
Madame Souflee I'm going to show you something. (*She takes out of her desk a little music box*) Whenever I get a little . . . homesick . . . I play this. (*She opens the box and it plays*)

The music for Song 14 begins

And when I hear this I feel as though I will be going home soon.

Song 14: Paris Paris

(*Singing*)   Paris, Paris, comme je vous aime
Sans vous je ne suis pas la même
Et quelquefois c'est vrai je pleure
Un petit peu, mais ce n'est pas mieux

Si quand j'écoute cette melodie
Je pense tout de suite à ma Paris
Les Champs Elysees dans la nuit
La tour Eiffel et la Pigalle

The last time that I walked along the Seine the sun was shining
I made a promise I'd be back before too long
I saw the old man selling boxes, pretty music boxes
And now I think of you each time I hear this song

Paris Paris alone am I
We never should have said goodbye
Forever you'll be home to me Paris, Paris.

Jessica and Madame Souflee walk off together

The Lights fade

Scene 6

The Examiner's office

Examiner (*shouting*) Next please.

Gill enters

Gill Good-afternoon sir.
Examiner Good-afternoon. Would you prefer to sit or stand?
Gill (*taking a seat*) Oh I'll sit if I may.

The Examiner listens to Gill's answer and writes it down, as he does with practically everything Gill says

Examiner (*to himself*) "Sit if I may". Good! Now if there were not a chair in here, then what? Would you prefer to sit or stand then?
Gill (*slightly hesitant*) I would still prefer to sit, although that alternative would not be open to me.
Examiner (*writing, saying to himself*) "Open to me". Good. Now. (*He looks up*) Is this a question?
Gill (*thinking for a second then, hesitantly*) Only if this is an answer.
Examiner (*to himself*) "An answer". Now, I see you wish to read law and philosophy?
Gill Yes sir.
Examiner Why have you not chosen to read "gardening"? Don't you like gardening?
Gill Yes sir. I do like gardening, but felt that I wasn't "down to earth" enough for it.
Examiner (*to himself*) "Down to earth". (*He looks up*) That's very good. (*He chuckles*) "Down to earth". Right. Stand up please.

Gill stands

Now. Where has your lap gone?
Gill (*thinking*) My lap ... my lap is more of a hypothetical area than a physical portion of my body. It describes the place where one's clothes automatically fold when one is in a sitting position.
Examiner (*writing and not looking up*) Thank you. Sit down please.

He now startles Gill by suddenly kicking his right leg high in the air several times, and at the same time nodding his head wildly

What am I doing now?
Gill (*flabbergasted*) I would say that you were kicking your right foot approximately two feet off the floor every three seconds, whilst, at the same time, managing to co-ordinate the sudden violent movement of the head to the right, consecutively with the foot movement.
Examiner (*still kicking wildly*) Continue! Continue! I would like another fifteen seconds at least on the subject.
Gill Another fifteen seconds ... well ... what can I say ... yes. This unusual movement is one I have never actually seen before although ... although it does remind me of that rather successful television personality John Cleese, in fact on thinking about it, this whole interview reminds me of a sketch from *Not The Nine O'clock News* or *Monty Python*, because ... because I honestly find it very hard to believe that for the last few years of my life I have been working ... NO ... sweating, worrying; not sleeping and praying that I'd be given a chance to go to this wonderful university. And then, when the great day comes for me to be given that chance, I'm

Act II, Scene 7

not asked what I think of the current world situation; about the economy of this country ... or even about my hobbies ... ambitions or thoughts. Oh no! I'm asked to describe some idiotic gesture that I wouldn't expect from a chimpanzee in the zoo. Well, you've had your fifteen seconds, but I'm sorry sir, this is what I think of your interview! (*She picks up a vase with flowers from the desk and pours it over his head*)

Examiner Thank you Miss Thorn. You will be notified in due course whether you are acceptable to the university. Goodbye.

Gill turns and leaves the room

Next please!

As the Lights go out we see the Examiner making a stupid gesture to the next applicant

SCENE 7

The classroom

The girls are all gathered around Gill. From outside the door is heard a wild scream. The girls look in the direction of the doorway and are shocked to see ...

Jessica reeling at the door, ashen-faced, a piece of paper clutched in her hand

Jessica Aaaaaaaaaaaaaaaaaaaaah!
Susie Jessica! What's the matter! Are you in pain!
Jessica Aaaaaaaaaaaaaaaaaaaaah!
Gill Let's sit her down. She looks terrible.

The girls help her to a chair with great difficulty

Helen May I say something?
Jessica (*shaking her head*) Aaaaaaaaaaaaaaaaaaaaah!
Cathy Jessica! What is it? What on earth's got into you? (*She notices the piece of paper in Jessica's hand, takes it and reads it*)Aaaaaaaaaaaaaaaah! (*She takes a seat next to Jessica, looking blankly into space*)
Susie Don't you start! Now look Cathy. I've always watched those bits in films when someone gets hysterical and they have to slap them round the face ... and I've always thought "I'd like to do that". Don't make me realize my ambition Cath!
Cathy OK, OK. I'll talk, I'll talk ... (*Dazed*) Twenty six thousand seven hundred and nineteen pounds! P. Stodgy have just discovered the largest deposit of gold since nineteen oh eight. Their shares have hit twelve pounds and they're still climbing. We're rich.

The girls scream and shout in panic

Susie My God! What are we going to do?

Helen May I say something?

Silence! The girls are waiting for her to talk Helen cannot understand it

I said, "May I say something?"
Gill Well, get on with it. What have you got to say? Believe me, any ideas at the moment are welcomed — even from you.
Helen You mean it! I can really talk! ... You really wanna hear what I was going to say.
Girls (*shouting in unison*) Yes!
Helen I don't believe it! I've forgotten! Don't worry, I'll remember ... just give me a mintue or two and it will come to me ...

The music for Song 15 begins

Song 15: Can I Say Something?

(*Singing*) Can I say something? Can I say something?
Something that is gonna set the world on fire.
You'll be confounded, and yes, astounded
I'm the kind of public speaker you admire.
See how you listen, my pearls of wisdom,
Seem to fall so gently on the crowds below.
But the only trouble is — I've one problem and it's this
What I'm talking about I don't really know, no, no, no
What I'm talking about I don't really know.

Can I say something? A little something?
That will make you wish you'd listened all these years.
Can I enthrall you, and try to fool you?
So that when I'm finished you will give three cheers
Oh aren't I brilliant and so resilient?
I come bouncing back with stunning repartee
Now I know it sounds absurd, but I mean every single word
But what I'm talking about better not ask me, me, me, me.
Yeh, what I'm talking about better not ask me.

Encore

Can I say something? Can I say something?
I know Joan of Arc could make a speech or two
And Cleopatra, and Maggie Thatcher,
But you see I taught them everything they knew
Do I surprise you, and mesmerize you?
Would you follow me from here to Kingdom Come?
Am I not the main event, would you vote me President?
Don't you see I'm really talking out my
Girls Bum bum bum bum,
Helen But I'm having such a terrific load of fun.

Act II, Scene 7

Possible encore

> Can I say something. Can I say something?
> When they gave me this part I was quite aghast
> 'Cos I'm a shy girl, a very shy girl
> I said "Try another member of the cast"
> Unlike Ralph Reader I'm not a leader
> And I find it very hard to scream and shout
> But as you probably can see, I have found a whole new me
> Barbra Streisand you had better just watch out out out out
> 'Cos I'm learning what "theatre's" all about.

Jessica Phew! After that I think we'd better let the girl talk. Come on Helen, out with it. What do you think we should do?
Helen I think we should own up.
Susie What!
Cathy She's mad!
Jessica No, let her talk. Go on Hel.
Helen Well, I know that what we've done isn't right. But we haven't hurt anybody have we? And Jess. Your mother's a good sport, she'll understand. Probably did the same type of thing when she was young. And as far as the bank's concerned, well, they've made money on the commissions, and Miss Betterby? That's the best part. Maybe we'll all get expelled!

The girls laugh and cheer

Jessica You know. I think Helen's right. That's what we should do. And there's no time like the present. I'm going to phone my mother now and confess all. I can assure you all that she'll be very understanding. (*She walks over to the school phone and dials*) You see, I know how to handle my mother. She just likes the cold, hard facts presented to her. She'll completely under—Oh hello Mother! It's Jessica ... (*She pauses*) JESSICA LANG, your daughter. Remember me? ... Good ... No everything's fine—well— there is one thing I wanted to discuss with you. (*She takes a deep breath and speaks very matter-of-factly*) The girls of six-C recently wanted to play a little joke on the school and Mr Duff at the bank and to make the joke work I'm afraid it was necessary for me to impersonate your voice and open another bank account—supposedly for you. The class then listened in to a few of our fathers' business conversation and started to invest in the Stock Exchange. I am please to be able to tell you tha——

Jessica holds the phone away from her ear and the sound of Jessica's mother's voice screaming away is heard in the background. It suddenly stops and Jessica replaces the receiver

Helen Gee, your mother's a good sport!
Gill You sure know how to handle your mother, Jess.

Cathy I guess she didn't do the same kind of thing when she was our age. What did she say, Jess?
Jessica Well, I'm sure you won't mind if I just give you the gist of her side of the conversation. She said she's never heard of such deceit, dishonesty, fraud, misrepresentation, malpra——
Cathy Right! Right! We get the idea. What's she going to do about it?
Jessica She's telephoning Miss Betterby and Mr Duff now!
Gill OK, Helen. Next bright idea please?
Helen Just one more thought! Is any one of the girls in Six-C studying prison reform?

A First-former rushes in

First-former You've all got to go and see Miss Betterby immediately.
Girls Oh! Oh!

The Lights fade

SCENE 8

Miss Betterby's office

Seated are Miss Betterby, Mr Duff, Sergeant Lawman and the teaching staff. The girls of 6C are standing

Miss Betterby ... Absolutely disgraceful! Before you came in I had a long telephone conversation with Mrs Lang—Jessica's mother. (*Looking at Jessica*) And I made sure it *was* your mother I was talking to! I explained to her that because she had made a complaint to the bank, the bank were forced to bring in the police and the police were obliged to bring in the school. Girls! I can't think what came over you. How could you do this to Edwina? What have you got to say?

The music for Song 16 begins

Song 16: Sorry

Susie	Sorry
Jessica	Sorry
Cathy	Sorry
Gill	Sorry
Helen	Sorry
Susie	You see, it's really my fault, but it started as a game,
Jessica	No it was me who thought it out, so I'm the one to blame
Cathy	Don't listen to a word now, it's simple—don't you see? They're trying hard to lie to you to cover up for me!
Susie	Sorry
Jessica	Sorry

Act II, Scene 8   47

Cathy	Sorry
Gill	Sorry
Helen	Sorry

Susie	I'm ready and quite willing, to pay for what I've done
Jessica	And I've always thought a year or two in prison might be fun
Gill	(Now) who really needs to go to university anyway? Especially after seeing my examiner yesterday.

Susie	Sorry
Jessica	Sorry
Cathy	Sorry
Gill	Sorry
Helen	Sorry

> Let me speak for the others, and make it very plain
> A blot against us now would leave an everlasting stain.
> We've got our lives before us, we're barely in our prime
> Can't you find it in your hearts to forgive us just this time?

All	Sorry
	Sorry
	Sorry
	Sorry
	Sorry

Miss Betterby Look! I wonder... if we could be... (*searching for the right word*) ... "sensible" about all this, then perhaps we could all benefit.

Mr Duff Benefit! I can't see any way that we could "benefit" from this rotten mess.

Miss Betterby Very well. Let me explain. Mrs Lang might benefit by not having her daughter sued for fraud. Sergeant Lawman here might benefit from having the undying gratitude of a member of staff.

Miss Nelson looks at Lawman and stands beside him

> The school might benefit under a provision in the law that really applies to employees of a firm earning money whilst in employment—but I'm sure this could quite easily be applied to schoolchildren ... and the bank ... (*she looks at Mr Duff*) ... the bank might benefit in a way that I can only leave to Mr Duff's imagination.

Mr Duff I say drop it! Drop the whole thing! If Mrs Lang is prepared to forget all about it, then I can assure you that the Listening Bank has listened and understood!

Miss Betterby Well, I can tell you that Mrs Lang has agreed with me that the whole episode is best forgotten completely ... except we don't want to forget to let the school have a cheque for ... how much is it now girls?

Helen Forty-one thousand three hundred pounds Miss Betterby.

Miss Betterby (*forgetting herself*) Oh! You clever little girls! ... (*Seriously*) Very naughty! ... (*Smiling*) But very very clever! (*Looking at the teachers in the room*) You see? I told you something would turn up didn't I?

Lawman Well, I suppose that about wraps things up. I must say I didn't think it would all end up as happily as this!

Mr Duff Good! Well back to work I suppose. (*After a pause*) Just one thing? What made you call the account T.D.A.L. ...? What do those letters stand for?

Jessica Oh! (*She looks around from one face to another*) Ummm ... Why! They stand for Edwina Roach's motto. THINK, DEVELOP AND LEARN!

Miss Betterby Oh you clever girls!

The Lights fade

Scene 9

The school hall

All the teachers and girls are on stage

Miss Betterby ... And now for our "Top Achievement" Award. As you know, this award was set up by Edwina Roach and is given to the girl with the best university pass. This year the award goes to Gill Thorn who got into Charterhouse College Cambridge.

The school cheer whilst Gill collects her award from Miss Betterby

Well, it's been a strange and very active year for Edwina Roach. Our standard of passes into universities has been excellent; we're about to start a most extensive building and repair programme for the school ... thanks to a most charitable donation; Miss Nelson is soon to become Mrs Lawman and, as I'm sure the school gossip machine will already know, I am about to become a Duff.

The school cheers

Let us end the term, as is the custom of the school with the School Song.

A song sheet is lowered for the whole school (audience) to sing to

Song 17: School Song (Reprise)

School   We love our school, we thank our school
For showing us the way
To love our country and our Queen
Yes caring day by day
We chose our school to find the road
That leads to morning light
We love our school we thank our school
For teaching what is right

Act II, Scene 9

> What a lot of old rot
> What a load of old rot
> We have to sing
> Love our country and our Queen
> What they're saying doesn't mean a single thing
> We didn't choose this school we put up such a fight
> We love our school we thank our school
> Let's burn it down tonight!

Song 18: Can We Say Something? (Reprise)

Company
> Can we say something? Can we say something?
> It's been really great tonight doin' this show
> Has it been funny and worth the money
> Could you leave a little more before you go
> We're so excited and so delighted
> That you came along to watch our little farce
> Will you tell your friends to come
> 'Cos they'll have a lot of fun
> If they don't mind spending two hours on their
> (*Wagging fingers*) A   AA   A
> If they don't mind spending two hours on their ...

CURTAIN

FURNITURE AND PROPERTY LIST

Only essential props are listed here; further dressing may be added at the discretion of the director and as facilities permit.

ACT I

SCENE 1

On stage: Portrait on wall
Dais

SCENE 2

On stage: Desks
Teacher's desk
Chairs
Blackboard

Personal: **Cathy:** prospectus in pocket
Miss Nelson: handkerchief

SCENE 3

On stage: Desk. *On it:* pen, forms, papers
2 chairs
Waste-paper basket

Personal: **Miss Nelson:** handbag with 2 photographs, compact with mirror

SCENE 4

On stage: Desk
2 chairs
Briefcase with papers for **Mr Duff**

SCENE 5

On stage: 2 chairs
Portrait on wall

SCENE 6

On stage: As Scene 1, plus:
Pay telephone

Share and Share Alike 51

Personal: **Jessica:** wrist-watch
Other girl: coin
Girls: copies of *Financial Times* and other newspapers in pockets

ACT II

Scene 1

On stage: Ballroom sign

Personal: **Miss Nelson:** handbag

Scene 2

On stage: As Act I, Scene 2, plus:
Financial newspapers on desks
Chalk and duster by blackboard

Personal: **Jessica:** bank statement, note in pocket

Scene 3

On stage: As Act I Scene 1

Personal: **Miss Betterby:** results in envelope
Mr Duff: pipe and matches in pocket

Scene 4

On stage: As Act I Scene 3

Personal: **Lawman:** Wrist-watch

Scene 5

On stage: As Act I Scene 2, plus:
Book for **Cathy**
Music box (practical) in teacher's desk

Scene 6

On stage: Desk. *On it:* papers, pens, vase of flowers
2 chairs

Scene 7

On stage: As Act I Scene 2, plus:
Pay telephone

Off stage: Piece of paper **(Jessica)**

Scene 8

On stage: As Act I Scene 4, plus:
Several chairs

SCENE 9

On stage: As Act I Scene 1, plus:
Award for **Miss Betterby**

Off stage: Song sheet **(Stage Management)**

LIGHTING PLOT

Only essential cues are listed; further cues may be added at the discretion of the director, and as facilities permit.

Property fittings required: *nil*

Various simple settings—several interiors and one exterior

ACT I, SCENE 1

To open: General interior lighting

Cue 1	**Girls** exit, curtain lowers *Concentrate lighting on teachers in front of curtain*	(Page 4)
Cue 2	**Miss Betterby** (*singing*): "... turn up, in the end." *Fade to black-out*	(Page 6)

ACT I, SCENE 2

To open: General interior lighting

Cue 3	**Jessica:** "... Something Will Turn Up!" *Fade to black-out*	(Page 10)

ACT I, SCENE 3

To open: General interior lighting

Cue 4	**Miss Nelson** (*singing*): "... funny feeling 'bout you." *Fade to black-out*	(Page 13)

ACT I, SCENE 4

To open: General interior lighting

Cue 5	**Miss Betterby** (*taking the notes; exaggeratedly*): "Thank you John." *Cross-fade to girls outside Miss Betterby's office*	(Page 16)
Cue 6	**Girls** shrug and walk off *Cross-fade to Miss Betterby's office*	(Page 16)
Cue 7	**Miss Betterby:** "... down the middle!" *Fade to black-out*	(Page 17)

ACT I, SCENE 5

To open: General interior lighting

Cue 8   At end of Song 6 (Page 20)
        Fade to black-out

ACT I, SCENE 6

To open: General interior lighting

No cues

ACT II, SCENE 1

To open: Exterior evening light

Cue 9   **Miss Nelson:** "... have a police escort!" (Page 27)
        Fade to black-out

ACT II, SCENE 2

To open: General interior lighting

Cue 10 At end of Song 9 (Page 31)
        Fade to black-out

ACT II, SCENE 3

To open: General interior lighting

Cue 11 At end of Song 12 (Page 35)
        Fade to black-out

ACT II, SCENE 4

To open: General interior lighting

Cue 12 **Miss Nelson:** "... very nice indeed." (Page 38)
        Fade to black-out

ACT II, SCENE 5

To open: General interior lighting

Cue 13 At end of Song 14 (Page 41)
        Fade to black-out

ACT II, SCENE 6

To open: General interior lighting

Cue 14 **Examiner:** "Next please!" (Page 43)
        Fade to black-out

Share and Share Alike 55

ACT II, SCENE 7

To open: General interior lighting

Cue 15 **Girls:** "Oh! Oh!" (Page 46)
   Fade to black-out

ACT II, SCENE 8

To open: General interior lighting

Cue 16 **Miss Betterby:** "Oh you clever girls!" (Page 48)
   Fade to black-out

ACT II, SCENE 9

To open: General interior lighting

No cues

EFFECTS PLOT

ACT I

Cue 1	**Girls** (*singing*): "... away two terms ago!" *Bell rings*	(Page 7)
Cue 2	**Girls** (*singing*): "... jabber off to France." *Bell rings*	(Page 8)
Cue 3	**Girls** (*singing*): "... the school bell ring?" *Bell rings*	(Page 8)

ACT II

Cue 4	During Scene 1 *Music for inside ballroom*	(Page 25)
Cue 5	**Jessica** holds telephone away from her ear *Muted voice of Mother screaming away in background—cut after a few seconds*	(Page 45)

www.ingramcontent.com/pod-product-compliance
Ingram Content Group UK Ltd.
Pitfield, Milton Keynes, MK11 3LW, UK
UKHW021847210426
5322IPUK00022B/523